The Easy Way To Start Internet Marketing

Disclaimer

This e-book has been written for information purposes only. Every effort has been made to make this eBook as complete and accurate as possible. However, there may be mistakes in typography or content. Also, this e-book provides information only up to the publishing date. Therefore, this eBook should be used as a guide - not as the ultimate source.

The purpose of this eBook is to educate. The author and the publisher do not warrant that the information contained in this e-book is fully complete and shall not be responsible for any errors or omissions. The author and publisher shall have neither liability nor responsibility to any person or entity with respect to any loss or damage caused or alleged to be caused directly or indirectly by this eBook.

About the Author

Jan Erik Horgen is an entrepreneur living in Norway who loves sharing knowledge and helping others on the topic of Internet Marketing.

Jan Erik is a dedicated person who will go the extra mile to deliver what you need in an efficient way.

Jan Erik's words of wisdom:

"I believe that knowledge is power. Everyone should improve themselves and/or business, no matter what stage in life they're in. Whether it's to develop a better mindset or to increase profits. Moving forward is key."

If you would like to learn more about Internet Marketing, please visit the following resources with very valuable free training (and a sales pitch of course...):

http://gohere2show.me/cbu

https://gohere2show.me/KBB

https://gohere2show.me/jcr

Published by:

Quintessence Publishing

November 2019

Contents

Disclaimer 2

About the Author 3

Introduction 6

Chapter 1-- How to Choose a Niche to Target. 7

    What is a Niche and Why Does it Matter? 7

    Why You Should Get More Specific When Choosing Your Niche. 8

    The Power of Creating Your Own Niche. 8

    Websites That Don't Fit Nicely Into Boxes. 9

    Bringing Various Concepts Together. 9

    Going More Niche. 9

    Trailblazing. 10

Chapter 2-- How to Choose a Business Name, Register a Domain, And Web Hosting. 11

    Choosing Your Domain Name and Site Name. 11

    Branding. 11

    Memorability. 11

    Individuality. 12

    Other Considerations. 12

    Buying Hosting and a Domain Name. 12

    WordPress. 13

    Begin With the Most Basic Promotion. 13

Chapter 3-- Email Marketing. 15

    What is Email Marketing? 15

    Utilizing Email Marketing. 16

    How to Get Your Emails to Stand Out. 16

    Receptivity. 16

    Images and Clickability. 17

Chapter 4 - Traffic Through Paid Advertising 18

The Goal of PPC Marketing..18

Designing Your Ad Accordingly 19

Targeting 19

Chapter 5 - How to Integrate Social Media to Grow Your Business. 20

Social Media Marketing Explained. 20

The Strategy. 20

How to Grow Your Connections..21

How to Improve Your Posts..22

Don't Give Up! 22

Chapter 6 - How to Start Monetizing. 23

Money making Methods for Your Website. 23

Ad Networks:..23

Affiliate Products. 24

Your Own Products and Services. 24

Producing and Selling an eBook. 25

Filter Visitors. 25

Chapter 7 - Growth Hacks and Advanced Strategies to Skyrocket Your Business...26

Development Hacks. 26

Guest Posts. 26

Usage Trending Hashtags. 26

Influencer Marketing. 27

Develop Link Bait. 27

Advanced Strategies. 27

Conclusion. 28

Introduction

So, you want to get started with online marketing? As an internet online marketer, you'll be able to generate income from the comfort of your home, without any limit as to how far you can scale and grow your service. It's highly satisfying, and it's an ability that you can utilize to land tasks, or market to other business, too.

In other words, you've made a great choice!

Maybe you've seen pals, or individuals online who appear to be earning cash from the comfort of their home-- and doing extremely well at it. Now it's time to try yourself!

There's just one issue: it's all rather complicated. If you're not acquainted with the world of online marketing, then you might even be questioning how it's even possible to generate income online without offering anything physical! It appears like everybody is promoting each other and no one is in fact delivering any physical products.

Then there is all the jargon: PPC, affiliate marketing, show ads, SEO, SMO, CTR, CPA ...

It's all a bit complicated and it's definitely unclear how or where to begin. Continue reading then, and we'll have a look at whatever you require to understand in order to become a master of internet marketing and to start making lots of money online.

Chapter 1-- How to Choose a Niche to Target.

The initial step to creating an online company is to select what kind of online company you want to develop. This begins by choosing a niche-- what is the subject matter you will be handling?

In this chapter, you will discover how to do this, and you will see how this initial decision goes on to influence every other action.

What is a Niche and Why Does it Matter?

Every website must have a specific niche which explains the example that you will be writing about and the people you will be writing it for. Your site might be a 'basic' site or an individual blog that doesn't stick to any specific subject, but even then, there will be at least a 'theme' or a feel connecting it together. You might discuss books, coffee and the city, however that's still a niche in its way and it's one that will attract an extremely specific type of person.

If you hope to be able to make a success of your site and knowing and comprehending your specific niche is extremely crucial. Too lots of web designers do not truly totally comprehend their niche and their sites tend to suffer as a result.

Basically, you should know what your specific niche is. For most website owners or blog writers this will be an extremely easy concern to respond to: the website will most likely be about 'football' or 'technology' which's relatively easy to specify.

If your website is more basic though, then make a list of all the subjects that you blog about routinely and then consider a) what ties them together, and b) what kind of person will read them. You've most likely developed a new specific niche on your own, but as long as your future material satisfies those very same criteria then you will be on the cash.

The specific niche you pick must primarily be identified by your own interests. This NEEDS to be something you're keen to discover and compose about if you're going to be living and breathing your blog for the next 10 years.

What's more, is that you will not be able to provide actually unique and valuable content if you don't understand anything about the subject! And hiring professional authors won't guarantee that you'll find somebody who has a genuine enthusiasm and interest for the topic.

While that's real, you likewise require considering the viability of the specific niche option. How competitive is it? Do you stand an opportunity against the greatest websites? How profitable and monetizable is it? We'll get onto this more in future chapters, however the topic you pick must be something that people want to invest money on and that has great deals of chances for informational products.

Because there is so much money to be made on that topic, Finance is the very best specific niche in this regard. However also, you'll find that you can make a great deal of cash blogging about dating, fitness, or other subjects that speak to a basic human requirement in this way.

Why You Should Get More Specific When Choosing Your Niche.

But in order to really succeed-- and to gain an edge over the competition - you need to go a little deeper. Sure, your site might be an innovation website, however what sort of technology do your blog about? Who are you writing for? And what is the purpose of your website?

For instance, you may discuss all sort of technology however discover that you seem to stick more to innovation that's just around the corner. Maybe you write great deals of big previews for technology that's coming. And perhaps you write in a very technical manner in which is clearly targeted at individuals who understand their stuff?

This is a very different specific niche from a website that evaluates standard business technology in a design that can attract the typical client.

You might make a football website sure, however is it a dry website that deals with an in-depth introduction of football for real fanatics? Or is it a more gossip filled website that's aimed at the normal 'bloke'?

If you can be consistent with your precise niche, then you will find that your site uses something that not every other site does. You will have a particular audience and individuals who particularly like the method you approach the subject. Stick to your guns and you can make your site extremely successful as a result.

The Power of Creating Your Own Niche.

That said however, there are couple of specific niches left that have a great variety of people interested but that however don't have too much overcrowding in the market. This is particularly difficult when you consider how important it also is that you in fact have an interest in the specific niche that you're going to be handling so regularly from now on and that you actually know a thing or two about it too.

So how do you standout without limiting your appeal or blogging about something dull? Well one solution is to come up with your own niche and to develop a site that will be unlike any other. Here we will look at how you can possibly accomplish that.

Websites That Don't Fit Nicely Into Boxes.

When you browse the web for motivation on specific niches for your website, you will often find lists of classifications such as 'fitness', 'generating income', 'football', 'film' and others like these. Not every site however has to fit nicely into a category like this - it is possible to come up with a completely special angle and to produce a niche that wasn't there prior to.

Take http://www.lifehacker.com for instance and http://www.lifehack.org. These websites exist in the same niche but return a decade which specific niche would not have existed. These sites loop great deals of themes using a 'way of living' or 'attitude' to gel it all together. In this case that attitude is the 'hacker' attitude - where DIY applies to whatever from self-improvement to making money; but you might just as quickly construct a site around any other central idea like this.

Bringing Various Concepts Together.

If you can't discover a new theme to link the items on your site though, then another alternative is to just integrate multiple existing specific niches that you think will go well together. Simply taking a wider technique with your stories can help to give your site more meat and put your niche more in context with other subjects.

This method is likewise effective due to the fact that it produces a variety of easy marketing options that you can utilize to reach a brand-new audience. For example, if you have a website based around bodybuilding and self-improvement, then you will have the ability to promote your website on self-improvement forums without being directly in competitors with those sites.

Going More Niche.

In contrast to widening your specific niche, another alternative is to get back at more specific by discovering a classification within a category. Once again, this will permit you to market on websites that would otherwise see you as competition and will assist make SEO much easier by focusing your objective. An example might be to target a particular type of movie such as '80s action films', a specific era of music, or perhaps a specific type of exercise such as bodyweight training alone.

Trailblazing.

Lastly, if you have the resources, then you can even think about creating a specific niche before you create your website. Then, if you run a software application business and you launch a new piece of software or a new computer system video game, then you will likely find that this produces interest and fans. By creating a site focusing on the software application you have actually released, you can then provide a main site for that interest and develop a practically cooperative relationship between your software application and your website where the success of one helps the success of the other. This works for every sort of product and service that will capture the public's attention. Not every webmaster will have an item to promote, it's essential that services and entrepreneurs don't miss this chance when it does present itself.

Chapter 2-- How to Choose a Business Name, Register a Domain, And Web Hosting.

Now you have your specific niche, it's time to turn that standard subject into a company design. This is where things can get complicated for some, but it's also the most fun and amazing part!

And all of it starts with picking your business name, which is extremely likely to likewise be your website name, which is extremely likely to likewise be your domain name (the address that visitors type into the browser to discover your website!).

Choosing Your Domain Name and Site Name.

If you are preparing to release a brand-new site, then there are numerous things you will need to do in preparation before you can even begin to think about content composing or SEO. Obviously among the most fundamental starting points is to discover a hosting service and to pick a domain name for your website or blog. This will offer you somewhere to save the files that make up your site, and it will offer your visitors a way to access them.

However, choosing a domain is more than just a useful matter, it's likewise going to have a big effect on the way your visitors view your website, and on the way, you'll go about promoting it. Here we'll look at how to pick a domain name that will make good sense from an organization perspective, and from an imaginative one too.

Branding.

Creating a name for your website that you can construct a brand around makes a great deal of sense for a number of reasons. For one, Google has explicitly specified that it will be attempting to offer more prominence to brand names and to bury 'precise name domains' (keyword URLs) in an attempt to reveal better quality websites. At the same time though, if you can develop a brand name this will give you more chance for future growth significance that you can more quickly market your site and produce awareness while utilizing that exact same branding in your marketing.

Memorability.

Obviously if you want individuals to come to your website often and to get the word out, then it likewise makes good sense to select a URL that will be simple to remember. Or to tell others about it if your website name is too long or ridiculous then this will suggest that individuals struggle to return to your site. Prevent complex combinations of dashes and underscores and attempt to make the URL as memorable as possible.

Individuality.

While Google is no longer providing any advantage to exact-name-domains, typing your URL into Google is still one way that people are most likely to get to your website. If your URL isn't at all distinct though, then you'll be buried someplace around page 100. In this regard then, calling a business 'Apple' would be a misstep (thankfully the Apple currently had a great deal of clout behind them).

Likewise having a more distinct business name will help you to be more remarkable again and will likewise help you to prevent utilizing any trademarked names. Obviously, you might also wish to do some research to guarantee that the name you want is offered and that you're legally entitled to use it. Having a special domain will likewise permit you to buy up similar domains (for typos and so on) with less opportunity of them currently being taken.

Other Considerations.

There are lots of more factors to consider bearing in mind besides these points though the degree to which they apply to your website will vary. Examine that there are no sites that have really similar names, and likewise do a search for trademarks to make sure that yours is unique (https://www.uspto.gov/trademark).

Buying Hosting and a Domain Name.

Now you have a name for your website, the next step is to develop it. This means doing a few things:

- Investing in a webhost.

- Buying your domain.

- Creating the basic foundation of your website.

A webhost is where your site will be kept. Popular alternatives consist of:

- Bluehost -- https://gohere2show.me/bluehost

- 10xHosting -- https://gohere2show.me/10xhosting

- HostGator -- https://gohere2show.me/hostgator

All of these will supply what you need to start, though our recommendation is to select Bluehost. A webhost essentially provides you with area on a huge, always-connected computer system called a server. You upload the files that constitute your site to this computer system, and then when somebody types your URL into the address bar, they will be shown those files.

That's why you also wish to buy the domain name. You can do this independently, but the bright side is that many webhosts will likewise permit you to buy a domain through their site straight away. As soon as you click that you want to register, this will be the first thing you do before you spend money on an offer.

When choosing a plan for your hosting, there are plenty of various options and settings. As you are beginning as a web marketer, you won't have a big quantity of traffic to begin with, and nor will you need to deal with great deals of huge files-- so the most fundamental options will do.

WordPress.

Lastly, you need to establish the basics of your website. To do this, I highly advise using WordPress.

WordPress is a completely totally free tool that is readily available on most hosting strategies and can be installed from the dashboard via a single click. This then provides you a skeleton website, and lets you quickly add brand-new posts, change a host of settings, and even set up totally brand-new styles and mini apps.

WordPress powers over a quarter of all sites on the internet, it is used by a lot of the best-known brand names on the planet, and it is entirely open-source and completely customizable. There is a substantial neighborhood of support (simply do a fast look for "how to establish a WordPress site" to get started), and it deals with the largest percentage of third-party apps and plugins. In other words, there is no reason not to use WordPress.

Begin With the Most Basic Promotion.

Over the next couple of chapters, we'll be looking at some sophisticated marketing and promo you can utilize to get your site to the top. This consists of social media marketing, e-mail marketing, and more. Prior to we get ahead of ourselves however, you may wish to simply begin occupying your website to get more people to go there.

Your job now then, is to find the blog area of your site and to add a new post that straight associates with your niche when every week to once every day (the more, the better). Merely adding more material to your website provides visitors a reason to keep inspecting back, to share your content, and to think about purchasing anything you're selling. Also, including material will assist to provide Google something to use to recognize the subject of your site, thereby assisting it to present your page when people look for relevant terms.

Keep in mind that you can do this a lot more effectively if you also utilize fundamental SEO. That means integrating search terms. This is an advanced form of marketing, but one that you can check out as you advance.

Chapter 3-- Email Marketing.

Now you have your website and a bit of content, it's time to begin actively marketing it-- to begin getting individuals to go there. How do you do that?

Among the most effective alternatives is email marketing, and this is where we're going to begin.

What is Email Marketing?

While social media have really grown recently, and SEO (that's Search Engine Optimization) has been through lots of changes that have actually lead individuals to question its dependability and effectiveness, e-mail marketing is something that has actually been around for the longest time and revealed no signs of going anywhere. Most of us will still begin our days by checking our email, and any messages we find in there are still likely to get read and discovered.

In order to get started with email marketing, you will first require getting something called an autoresponder. This is a tool that you utilize in order to gather email addresses and after that to send multiple messages at set times.

While you may believe this is something you can do without a subscriber list, that is never true. To effectively collect and handle emails, you will require to handle spam and ensure that people truly want to be on your list-- both of which will involve making use of a confirmation email. You'll likewise require handling people unsubscribing, you'll wish to maintain "list hygiene" by eliminating defunct e-mails, and you'll want to be able to track who opens your emails and which ones are most effective. None of this would be possible to do manually.

Consider the following autoresponders, the following two are currently the most popular, and are safe choices:

GetResponse	AWeber
https://gohere2show.me/getresponse	https://gohere2show.me/aweber

Other good options include: ConvertKit, Drip, MailChimp and ActiveCampaign, but my personal favorite is newcomer SendEagle, created by the most experienced email marketers around, to meet the needs of real email marketers. https://gohere2show.me/sendeagle

With this tool, you'll have the ability to produce a form to collect user information. You can then add this to your website in the sidebar, or at the bottom of each post. WordPress will let you do this easily with making use of plugins.

Utilizing Email Marketing.

When somebody lands on your website is a useful and powerful strategy for turning visitors into leads, collecting emails. Now you can market new items to them and motivate them to come back to your website.

One method to use your email marketing is to send e-mails that supply extra content-- similar to your post. Another choice is to email people speaking about all the posts you've recently contributed to your website in order to encourage them to visit again.

Then, when you have a product to offer, you will message to promote that item and drive more sales. This will be gone over in a subsequent chapter.

The point is that by using email marketing, you aren't relying on your visitors examining your site each and every single day. You now have a way to reach them-- and it's a manner in which isn't dependent on a third-party website like Google or Facebook.

How to Get Your Emails to Stand Out.

While email marketing has remained reliable, it has somewhat changed in the last decade or so-- even though it might not be obvious on the face of it. The greatest modification naturally is the manner in which we check our e-mails. For the majority of us, this is now done on the move and constantly through our smart devices and tablets. Rather than getting home and checking 20 emails at the same time, we are instead 'leak fed' emails throughout the day as we go about our organization.

This in turn then means that each e-mail will be most likely to 'stand out' from the others and get noticed by itself benefits, however it likewise indicates that we have ended up being more familiar with just brushing them off and viewing them as a nuisance. If you want your email marketing project to be a success, then you require to take that into consideration and factor it into the way you design your subject headings and the way you send your messages.

Receptivity.

When you produce your newsletter, you will choose the name of it based on who you believe will be receptive to your message. This ought to be a targeted newsletter so that individuals you are calling will find your product or service pertinent-- it's no excellent sending a Priest a catalogue of baby clothes.

What time are they getting home from work? Sending out materials on a Sunday early morning will be much more efficient than sending them at 3pm on a Monday-- so get as much information as you can about your recipients and consider the temporal factor in your marketing.

Oh, and if you can get your mailing list to agree to your marketing info you will discover that they are always far more responsive to what you need to say.

Images and Clickability.

You need to believe about the images you utilize in your message if you want to get your recipients to then purchase something or visit your website. Using a clickable button instead of a small link will always enhance your click through rate due to the fact that it will be more interesting press. Also, using images can help to make a quick visual impression on your visitors.

However, then you need to think about the fact that lots of e-mail accounts will obstruct images from unknown senders, which people can end up being annoyed by downloading big images. Keep your messages relatively plain then and use images sparingly to provide more impact. Thinking about the vast array of devices your message will be seen on will assist you to prevent restricting your effect.

Chapter 4 - Traffic Through Paid Advertising

PPC represents Pay Per Click and describes making use of ad networks such as Facebook Ads or AdWords in order to promote your site or item. Generally, with any of these services you agree to pay a set amount for each time someone clicks your advert and, in this manner, you can avoid spending money on a campaign that is not successful.

Still you require to consider how you are going to convert the traffic you acquire into revenue and you need to consider how you can get the right people to click the adverts. There are a variety of techniques to making an effective and most significantly a successful PPC project, so here we will take a look at what those are.

The Goal of PPC Marketing

This is really the most crucial thing to keep in mind; that a PPC campaign that gets the most clicks is not always the most successful one, as that means that you're in fact spending the most cash. You only desire people to click your adverts if they're likely to earn you money once they come to your website - if they're most likely to be returning visitors for example who will click your advertisements, or if they are most likely to buy the items that you are selling.

One of the very best methods to make use of your PPC campaign is to connect straight to a landing page where you are selling a product. Then if you can get the product to cost state $30 a toss, then you can afford to pay $1 per click as long as you offer to at least 1/3rd of your visitors (this is called a conversion rate). This way you are still making a profit.

Pay Per Click advertisements are shown based upon a split-second bidding system. That indicates that the more you opt to pay per "per click" (you get to set this amount), the more your advertisement will be displayed in the relevant spots. By increasing the conversion rate on your website and by enhancing the ads, you can invest more money and get your ad seen by more individuals - scaling up your profits.

In order to work with this then you require to focus much more on the CTR (Click Through Rate) on your page and the quality of the traffic that the PPC advertisement is bringing you. In fact, you're just wasting your cash if you are deceiving people into clicking your advert and they are then just investing a minute on your page. If your page isn't doing an excellent adequate job of persuading individuals to purchase, then again you are really tossing cash away.

Designing Your Ad Accordingly

As such you should be intending to develop an advert that will draw in the attention you want it to from the right people, and just if they are likely to buy.

In other words, then you can think about consisting of the rate in your advert, the factor being that this will then permit you to repel people who aren't ready to invest that sort of cash - which is simply great due to the fact that you don't wish to spend for them to come to your website.

What is essential still however is that your advert catches the eye so that individuals you wish to see it do, and the essential thing to bear in mind for this is that your advert MUST looks expert if you intend to make sales. Be professional, be sincere and be up front and then as long as you focus on the CTR of your landing page you can very dependably create cash this way.

Targeting

Whether you select to use Facebook Ads or Google AdWords, one of the most essential considerations for an effective campaign is targeting. To put it simply, your e-mails reaching the right people - the people who are likely to buy from you. Once again, this increases the conversion, indicating that you can invest more money, meaning that you increase your revenues.

AdWords shows adverts on Google's search engines and is based upon what people search for. You will choose the search terms you wish to target, and when someone looks for that phrase, your advertisement will appear at the top as a "sponsored result."

Facebook Ads shows advertisements on a user's Facebook homered based on their interests, demographics, and more. You can in this manner choose to reveal your physical fitness book just to individuals who have actually listed "working out" as an interest (but who may also have listed their weight as being a little on the heavier side!).

Keep in mind though, that while Facebook lets you target an audience based on a higher quantity of details, Google lets you target people based on their intent. In other words, if someone searches for "buy fitness eBook," then that informs you that they are in fact looking to buy an eBook.

If you are attempting to make your cash from advertisements though (and once again, we'll discuss this alternative quickly), you might not have the ability to funnel as much cash into your organization plan.

Chapter 5 - How to Integrate Social Media to Grow Your Business.

Now you have PPC and e-mail marketing being utilized to direct traffic to your site, and to drive sales of an item (that we have not included yet). However, there are still more tools available for driving a lot more customized.

One such tool is social media. Social media is a very helpful resource when it comes to getting traffic because it essentially lets you talk with an audience like a human being. We all utilize social media, and so we understand how it ticks. This is definitely NOT necessarily true of Google!

What also makes social networks effective, is that it lets you develop relationships with your audience. That in turn can be tremendously powerful when it pertains to getting people to end up being devoted to your site, getting them to register for your emails, and getting them to visit your page directly - Google or no!

Social Media Marketing Explained.
Often it can feel a little like guesswork when you're attempting to build a following on social networks - specifically when you start out.

Initially you'll feel like every post you compose is falling on deaf ears and after spending ages developing fascinating things to say you'll be met with the noise of silence in return. And what sort of content should you be focusing on anyway? And how do you get people to listen?

While it can seem like you're simply blindly fumbling about in the dark though, there is a proven approach for discovering success on social media and it's perfectly possible to systemize the process to guarantee quick success. Here we will look at how to execute the very best strategy and utilize the right tools to start producing a following and taking the uncertainty out of social networks marketing.

The Strategy.
When you understand how, the process of developing an effective social media project is relatively straightforward. The objective is to constantly provide value to your audience via fascinating and helpful posts that you upload regularly to your different accounts.

At the same time though, you likewise require making sure that you have a strong brand name identity throughout these accounts. That indicates that you need to have the very same account name, logo and imagery on Facebook and Tumblr as you do on Twitter and Instagram. You need to be creating several channels that your visitors can utilize to find you and utilizing them all synergistically.

From there you need to start constructing your fans. This is trickier when you're beginning as fans beget fans - to put it simply, individuals will be most likely to sign up when they see other people have.

To start those followers can be found in you need to make certain you have social networks buttons your site or blog. That does not just suggest sharing buttons - but links directly to your account that your visitors can follow to find you. You can utilize more sophisticated widgets to display your channels, such as having a Twitter feed (this will have the added bonus of making your site look more active).

This is extremely important and while you may not believe it would work, just having those links there will suffice to gradually get some visitors seeping in.

From there you keep posting. And you can utilize some of the following tools and strategies to begin getting even more followers as you do ...

Some fast tips:

- Use the most trending hashtags when publishing.

- If you can't be on every social platform (which is perfect), then attempt to be on the ones that fit your design of content development and that target the same audience that you are.

How to Grow Your Connections.

Wish to know among the greatest inspiring drives for individuals? A sense of obligation. That is to say that if someone feels like you've done something for them, they will feel forced to do something back till they feel like they've done as much for you.

This effective idea can be crucial in constructing your social media following. Simply add people and they will add you back. Or, retweet their posts and they will retweet yours. It really is that simple.

That said though, you do not want to squander your time adding millions of fans and after that retweeting their things if you aren't going to see any take advantage of it. That then is where a tool like Social Rank can come in extremely Handy - this will inform you which of your fans is engaging with you the most and which of them has the greatest following of their own. If you desire to understand who to retweet and who to engage with more typically, very effective things!

When it comes to your social media followers, what Social Rank also does is to highlight the value of quality over quantity. Simply put, it's better to have one influential and active fans than a million who don't care about you and do not have any reach of their own.

Even better, you wish to find individuals to add who are potential consumers - which is where something like NeedTagger (www.needtagger.com) comes in. This lets you discover people who are likely to be interested in your services or products!

How to Improve Your Posts.

As you post, you likewise need to guarantee you are monitoring how reliable those posts are so that you understand whether what you're doing is working.

LikeAlyzer (www.likealyzer.com) lets you see which of your Facebook posts succeed and what your competition is doing - along with providing you with actionable suggestions for your own page.

In general, make certain that your posts are utilizing popular hashtags which they're focused on hot subjects. BuzzSumo (www.buzzsumo.com) is a very useful tool that will enable you to quickly see what topics are currently popular while you can see trending tags on Twitter itself. You can likewise use tools like Buffer (www.buffer.com) to save you time in fact publishing (it lets you queue posts).

Don't Give Up!

Hopefully these pointers will have assisted you to start feeling more positive in your social media campaign. If you find you aren't a hit over night though don't worry - these things require time and a combination of experimentation and lots of information will just help you improve your strategy. This isn't an art, it's a science, and as soon as you get the hang of it it's an extremely powerful tool for you to take advantage of.

Chapter 6 - How to Start Monetizing.

If you got into this with the objective of generating income from your site ... then what are you waiting for? If you have people actively visiting your website and reading your material, then there are lots of ways that you can produce a terrific profit from that without needing to jeopardize in any major way and without even impacting the experience for them.

You'll earn money even as you sleep, and you'll find that you get wealthier without actually doing anything beginning as soon as you set it all up.

That's right, we're finally getting to that point. It's the internet marketing dream!

The only minor challenge between you and your delighted future of passive income is choosing which money-making technique to utilize and choosing how precisely you are going to turn your site into a cash cow. Here we will look at a few of the options readily available to you and their weak points and strengths.

And for the rest of you who are currently running effective profitable sites this still applies to you - as it might simply be that you aren't making the most of your site in that regard and you could stand to learn a thing or more.

Money making Methods for Your Website.

The following are some of the most powerful monetization techniques for any website. Simply remember that you don't necessarily need to select in between these. Often the very best method is to use them together!

Ad Networks:

That code then autogenerates adverts from participating marketers based on the content on your pages, and that in turn guarantees that you get the most relevant adverts revealing up on your sites and that you don't need to worry about chasing after down the marketers yourself. You will then be paid in most cases per click every time someone clicks on one of your advertisements.

The most apparent advertisement network that most people utilize is Google AdSense which is known for fairly high pay and is a reliable and simple to carry out system. Some companies make their entire living from AdSense.

However, AdSense is not the only advertisement network on the block, and there are some out there with slightly less rigid requirements (for all those of you who own betting sites) which are less most likely to just close down your account (as several webmasters have actually reported Google doing).

At the exact same time you may choose to integrate numerous advertisement networks. You can do this using AdSense if you are utilizing another comparable network, but if the method is adequately different then you can double up if you so desire - for instance you can utilize 'in text' ads such as Kontera.

Affiliate Products.

Offering affiliate products is typically more profitable on a per-click basis, but you will have a much lower conversion rate as people have to in fact put their money where their mouse is and buy something in order for you to get any advantage.

Amazon has possibly the most popular affiliate service permitting you to get a cut for recommending a range of their products. This is once again a relatively low cut, and you can get more from using.

more services. Most supplement stores for instance have an affiliate scheme if you are a webmaster, and Clickbank supplies a terrific method for you to find lots of other partners and sell such items as eBooks.

Your Own Products and Services.

If you are making cash in this way, what you require to acknowledge in all of these cases however without exception is that you are at the bottom of the stack. At the end of the day you are getting paid to send individuals far from your site, and as those advertisers want to do this that informs you that they deserve more than you are making money for them.

As such, the most reliable way to make money from a visitor is to offer services and products. Now you can do this by buying and selling items wholesale and making a little profit on each one, however this will require a great deal of time, administration and storage area. Better is to make that money by selling services and products that are totally free for you to mass produce.

The best example of this is to sell e-books and even print books (where you utilize POD services) which requires no work on your part once they have actually been set up. You can offer memberships to your website, copywriting and web services, or even a 'course' which might consist of some routine e-mails, a book and membership in one plan. And individuals will want to pay a lot for that if you market it well.

E-books use the most basic method to start generating income from your site right away though, so let's take a look at how you can begin making money in this manner firstly.

Producing and Selling an eBook.

Most of all, you likely want to make your own product. This can be a book, a course, a series of videos or a series of other things. The style here is up to you, but self-improvement of various kinds - such as dating, weight loss or cash making - are typically very lucrative. Make certain that you are really behind your product and you believe in it strongly, as this will help you to believe in your own marketing and to press it everywhere you can. You need a rethink your approach, if you're ashamed or shy regarding your own product.

Another idea is to think about your target market. Select one market and create your item specifically for them and you will have more success than more slightly intending your item at everyone. Think of your demographic and develop a fictional person in your mind that would be your ideal customer. As you design your product ask yourself - would 'Dave' like this?

Filter Visitors.

Now you want to have the ability to direct your visitors as needed in order to convert them from visitors into cash. Here's a fast concern that can often be highly illuminating regarding your site - when somebody first visits your web page, what do you want to be the first thing they do? If you presently can't answer that definitively, then you will discover your visitors do not understand where to go either.

This is what you must be wanting from your visitors: an e-mail address. A fantastic method to do this is to provide something away for complimentary.

Chapter 7 - Growth Hacks and Advanced Strategies to Skyrocket Your Business.

Now whatever is in place. Now you have an outstanding site developed in WordPress, with a clever branding and domain name. You have a style that is born out of the specific niche you chose, you have regular material coming out, and all of that content is directing your visitors to either buy an item, click an advertisement, or register to your subscriber list - you're generating income either way.

But that's simply the start. Now it's time to grow. And the good news is that there are some reliable and very quick methods to do this.

This chapter is going to share "growth hacks" and advanced methods. It's not simply going to share the normal slew. Rather, it's going to contain the techniques utilized by the most significant brands in the world, and the essential difference between a highly successful website, and one that simply turns over a little revenue before going under.

Development Hacks.

Growth hacks are methods you can utilize in order to get ahead when promoting a site. They essentially enable you to circumvent the normal steady trajectory for the appeal of a website and rather to develop a much steeper climb.

Here are some examples:

Guest Posts.

A guest post is a post that you write and give for free to another material creator. The idea is that this post then includes a link back to your site. They secure free content, but in exchange, you get a link that will enhance your ranking on Google AND lead to a lot of direct clicks from that creators' following. Not just is it a link but it will also serve as a testimonial of sorts from somebody those individuals trust!

Usage Trending Hashtags.

Especially when posting to social networks, this makes a substantial difference. If you're uncertain what hashtags to use, have a look at the ones used by your finest rivals.

Developing content based on present patterns can be an exceptionally helpful technique.

Influencer Marketing.

Influencer marketing is a strategy that involves getting somebody with a big following to mention your blog (typically called a shortcut). This works incredibly well, since you might get a click from state 10% of that individual's audience. That's a BIG influx of traffic right there if they have 1 million fans!

Develop Link Bait.

Link bait is a term for a post that is so helpful and such a terrific talking point, that you can practically ensure that people are going to start linking to it totally free and thus supplying you with complimentary traffic and a better credibility in the eyes of Google.

Good examples of link bait consist of posts that are complete guides to a topic, in addition to those that argue a questionable point.

Advanced Strategies.

Development hacks might be popular, but more important is to take your abilities to the next level and to develop the major, advanced methods used by major brands and blog sites.

An example of this is SEO. SEO can be extremely effective in helping you to acquire more visitors for your website, and particularly if you utilize SEO together with a large amount of material with affiliate links.

Some reliable and fast suggestions for good SEO:

- Use a tool like Keywordtool.io to find your search terms.

- Be subtle in your use of keywords when writing - 1% density is ample.

- Use related terms and synonyms.

- Include the keyword in your opening and closing paragraph, one header, and your page's title.

Another example of a sophisticated strategy is to develop a YouTube channel. This is one of the best ways to build a relationship with your visitors and to gain more exposure. It can be video game changing, if you make the effort to develop a successful channel.

Make sure that you invest a lot of time and effort on branding. The secret to an extremely successful brand is to make sure that as quickly as someone takes a look at your website or your logo, they know if it is going to interest them.

Conclusion.

This book has been teaching you about the basic tools and skills you require to begin your journey in online marketing.

What's more crucial is taking action. Because you are developing on your own platform, building your site is one of the most crucial things you can do to succeed online.

Use the social channels with SEO and paid advertising to gain an audience to your website, and promote quality offers to construct your brand name and company.

Most importantly, never ever stop finding out new ways to approach your market and give value. And remember: Those who are successful today started from the bottom at some point too.

www.ingramcontent.com/pod-product-compliance
Lightning Source LLC
Chambersburg PA
CBHW040304220526
45473CB00002B/578